YOU CHOOSE™

SURVIVAL

Can You Survive
IN THE
SPECIAL FORCES?

An Interactive Survival Adventure

by Matt Doeden

Consultant:
Raymond Puffer
Historian, Ret.,
Edwards Air Force Base
History Office

CAPSTONE PRESS
a capstone imprint

You Choose Books are published by Capstone Press,
1710 Roe Crest Drive, North Mankato, Minnesota 56003.
www.capstonepub.com

Library of Congress Cataloging-in-Publication Data
Doeden, Matt.
Can you survive in the Special Forces?: an interactive survival adventure /
by Matt Doeden.
p. cm. — (You choose: Survival)
Includes bibliographical references and index.
Summary: "Describes the fight for survival as a member of the U.S. Special Forces"—
Provided by publisher.
Audience: Grades 4–6.
ISBN 978-1-4296-8582-5 (library binding)
ISBN 978-1-4296-9480-3 (paperback)
ISBN 978-1-62065-379-1 (ebook PDF)
1. Special forces (Military science)—United States—Juvenile literature. I. Title.
UA34.S64D64 2013
356'.160973—dc23   2012004678

Editorial Credits
Angie Kaelberer, editor; Gene Bentdahl, designer; Wanda Winch, media researcher;
  Danielle Ceminsky, production specialist

Photo Credits
General Atomics Aeronautical Systems, Inc., 16; Newscom: epa/Erik S. Lesser,
6; U.S. Air Force Photo: SSGT Reynaldo Ramon, 93; U.S. Army photo: Staff Sgt.
Andrew Kosterman, 10; U.S. Marine Corps photo: Lance Cpl. Christopher M.
Carroll, 52; U.S. Navy Photo: Chief Journalist Robert Benson, 74, U.S. Navy Photo:
Mass Communication Specialist 2nd Class John Scorza, 98, U.S. Navy Photo: Mass
Communication Specialist 3rd Class, Petty Officer Blake Midnight, 8, 12, U.S. Navy
Photo: Photographer's Mate 2nd Class Eric S. Logsdon, 78; U.S. Navy Seal and SWCC,
cover, 70, 76, 83, 87, 100; U.S. Army and Special Operations Command (USASOC):
Fort Benning Public Affairs Office/Sue Ulibarri, 102, USASOC: U.S. Army Photo,
21, 24, 47, 57, 61, USASOC: U.S. Army Photo: Angelo Jasper, 33, Jessica Bruckert, 65,
Sgt. Daniel Love, 7th SFG(A) PAO, 34, Sgt. Marcus Butler, 55, Staff Sgt. Thaddius
Dawkins, 49th Public Affairs Detachment, 28; Trisha Harris, 42, 44

Printed in China.
001870

TABLE OF CONTENTS

About Your
ADVENTURE

YOU are a member of the U.S. Special Forces. As one of the nation's most highly trained soldiers, you're an important part of the U.S. military. You carry out the most difficult, dangerous missions around the world.

Chapter One sets the scene. Then you choose which path to read. Follow the directions at the bottom of each page. The choices you make will change your outcome. After you finish one path, go back and read the others for new perspectives and more adventures.

YOU CHOOSE the path you
take through your adventure.

Extraction ropes allow helicopters to quickly pull Rangers to safety.

CHAPTER 1

The Best and Brightest

The United States military is made up of nearly 1.5 million people. Many are infantry soldiers, sailors, pilots, engineers, or even cooks. A rare few serve under the U.S. Special Forces Operations Command.

Only the best and brightest soldiers even earn the chance to try out for these elite units. Fewer still make the cut. Congress officially bans women from serving in combat, so no women are Special Forces members.

Turn the page.

Navy SEAL training includes carrying huge logs.

The Special Forces Operations Command is composed of many specialized groups. They include the U.S. Army Special Forces (Green Berets), the Navy SEALs, the Army Rangers, the Air Force's 1st Special Operations Wing, the 160th Special Operations Aviation Regiment (Airborne), and the ultrasecret Delta Force.

Each group has its own specialties. The SEALs learn to fight on sea, air, and land. Army Rangers are trained to be the first troops into a combat situation. The Green Berets specialize in covert and psychological operations.

Special Forces members get the best training in the military. It's not for just any soldier. It's difficult, exhausting, and often brutal.

For example, Navy SEALs train for up to two years before they can join an operational unit. The hardest part of their training is Hell Week. For five and a half days, trainees are almost constantly challenged. They perform difficult physical and mental tasks and are allowed only about three or four hours of sleep during the entire time. Those who can't handle this brutal training must leave the program. Other Special Forces units have similar trials. Only the strongest men are able to complete the training and join the Special Forces.

Turn the page.

Special Forces training may involve mountain climbing.

Life doesn't get much easier after training. Special Forces are trusted with the nation's most difficult, deadly, and secret missions. They perform daring rescues, carry out attacks, and gather important intelligence about enemies of the United States. They rely on their training and on each other to survive seemingly impossible situations. Their goal is always to successfully complete their mission and return safely.

Do you have what it takes to survive in the Special Forces? Choose your mission to find out!

To join the Green Berets on a dangerous rescue mission, turn to page **13**.

To join the Army Rangers and seize an enemy airstrip, turn to page **43**.

To join the SEALs and try to capture a terrorist leader, turn to page **71**.

Many Special Forces missions take place under the cover of darkness.

CHAPTER 2

Green Berets: Quiet Professionals

The mission: Hostage rescue

Objective: Terrorists have taken five U.S. diplomats hostage. Your mission is to rescue all five hostages.

The enemy: At least a dozen well-armed terrorists in a heavily defended compound

Rules of engagement: Use deadly force as needed.

It's nighttime in the desert. You crouch down low behind a rocky ridge. You scan the horizon with a pair of night-vision goggles. You've just received intelligence that five U.S. diplomats are being held hostage by a terrorist group.

Turn the page.

The terrorists attacked a group of vehicles traveling across a rocky stretch of open desert. Now they're holding the hostages in a small compound. The kidnappers have sworn to kill the hostages unless the United States releases several imprisoned terrorists. The kidnappers believe that their location is a secret, but U.S. intelligence officers have discovered it. The clock is ticking. The hostages don't have much time.

You're in command of a team of 12 Green Berets. Your intelligence officer, 1st Lieutenant Joe Hicks, is by your side.

"This is the compound, Captain," he says. "The hostages are inside. There are two guards at the outer gate, and two more snipers on the roof. An informant reports that the hostages are being held in a bunker below the compound."

Time is critical. The terrorist group is known for killing hostages when they don't get their way. They have promised to start the killing in exactly one hour. You can't let that happen.

You call Warrant Officer Rob Martinez, your second-in-command. "What are our options?" you ask.

"We could call in an air strike and take out the gate and the snipers," he suggests.

An air strike would make things a lot easier and safer for your men. But there's no way to be sure the hostages are safe underground. That intelligence came from a local informant. You can't be sure it's accurate. If it's wrong, the air strike could kill the hostages. An air strike also would take away any element of surprise you might have.

To order the air strike, turn to page 16.

To try sneaking into the compound, turn to page 18.

The MQ-1 Predator shoots AGM-114 Hellfire missiles.

"Call in an air strike," you tell your communications officer, Sergeant Paul Evans. "We can make this job a whole lot easier if we take out those guards and snipers."

Within minutes a U.S. Navy MQ-1 Predator drone is in the air. The remotely piloted aircraft carries two small air-to-surface missiles. You and your men watch the terrorist compound as you wait for the Predator to arrive.

Moments before the air strike is scheduled to happen, one of your men notices movement outside the compound. A group of men is gathered near one of the building's outer walls. They seem to be dragging someone with them. You can't get a good look at the person, but it could be a hostage. You have to think fast.

*To call off the air strike, turn to page **20**.*

*To continue as planned, turn to page **22**.*

"We've got the element of surprise," you say. "We need to take advantage of it."

You order your men to surround the compound. You'll go in alone, trying to reach the hostages before the terrorists know you're there. Your men will storm the compound at the first sign of trouble.

When everyone is in place, you move. You stick to the shadows as you move toward an unwatched section of the chain-link fence surrounding the compound. It takes just a few minutes to cut through the fence and slip inside.

So far, so good. Nobody has seen you. You carefully sneak around the side of the building. You approach a window and peer inside. The room is dark and empty. You pull yourself up and silently drop inside. You hear voices in the hallway beyond a closed door. Like most Green Berets, you're an expert in languages. You understand what the enemy is saying.

"Take a hostage outside," one man says. "Let's show the Americans that we mean what we say."

They're planning an execution! You and your men have to act fast.

To open the door and shoot the men, turn to page **24**.

To wait until they've passed before moving, turn to page **26**.

"Abort! Abort the air strike!" you shout. Evans springs into action, relaying your orders to the base. You hold your breath for a few tense moments. You hope there was enough time to stop the Predator from firing. Evans looks up and gives you a nod. You let out your breath. That was close.

You watch the terrorists through night-vision goggles. They have forced a man into a chair. The man wears a hood over his head. It's almost certainly one of the hostages. One of the terrorists sets up what appears to be a video camera. Your gut churns as you realize what they're about to do.

"Captain," says Martinez.

"I see it," you say, cutting him off. You have to move now, or the hostage will be killed.

"I've got a shot, Captain," says Sergeant Chris Jones, your best sniper.

Green Berets perform missions in Afghanistan and other war-torn areas.

You trust that Jones will make the shot, but there are at least five terrorists outside. Killing one might cause the others to kill the hostage before you can rescue him.

To command your sniper to take the shot, turn to page 28.

To order your men to storm the compound, turn to page 31.

"Captain?" asks Evans, awaiting your order. After a moment of thought, you shake your head. "The Predator is almost here. It may be our best shot."

In less than a minute, the Predator passes overhead. It's so high that you don't see or hear it. Then the night sky lights up as two missiles smash into the compound.

"Report!" you shout as the smoke clears.

"Hostiles down," Martinez answers. "Two down at the gate and two more on the roof. Multiple down alongside the compound. If that was a hostage, he's probably dead."

You frown at the news about the hostage. But there's no time to worry about that now. "Move in," you order. The remaining terrorists are now unprotected.

You and your men break from cover and rush in. You face no resistance outside the compound. You signal Martinez to take your team's medic and check on the downed men outside the compound. "Try to take any surviving hostiles prisoner. If you find a hostage, do what you can to save him."

You kick in the door of the compound and go inside. You and the rest of your team carefully move through the hallways. There's a fire in one corner of the compound. The halls are filling with smoke.

As you round a corner, you stop suddenly. Before you stands a hostage. One of the terrorists holds him from behind. The terrorist holds a gun to the hostage's head. The message is clear. He'll shoot the man unless you lay down your weapon.

To take a shot at the terrorist, turn to page **34**.

To try to negotiate with the terrorist, turn to page **37**.

Green Berets secure and search enemy compounds.

You kick open the door, throw yourself into the hallway beyond, and take aim. With two quick shots, both enemies are dead. But the sound of gunfire has alerted the remaining enemies that you're there. Your team will have heard the shots as well. They'll attack, but you can't wait for help. Every second counts. You have to move.

You rush down the hallway and round a corner. But you suddenly pull up short. A terrorist is standing there, holding one of the hostages in front of him. He's using the hostage as a shield.

"You are too late," the terrorist says in broken English. "We already killed one of your diplomats. Drop that weapon, or I'll kill this one too."

You could take a shot, but it will be risky. You could hit the hostage. Or the terrorist could pull the trigger on his weapon before he falls.

To take the shot, turn to page **34.**

To try to negotiate with the terrorist, turn to page **37.**

The enemy still doesn't know you're here. You're not about to give up the element of surprise. Once the voices outside have faded, you quietly slip through the door. You're in a long hallway. A staircase leads down at one end. That has to be where the hostages are.

You creep silently down the hallway. A light shines dimly from the bottom of the steps. You hear muffled voices. You move down the steps with your back against the wall. From the bottom step, you peer around a corner. You see a large room. Four hostages are tied to chairs on the far wall. You spot two guards. Each is holding a pistol. Neither is looking toward the staircase, but they could turn around at any moment.

One of the hostages notices you. Lucky for you, she doesn't say a word. You make eye contact with her, then nod toward the two guards. She nods slightly in return. She understands that you want her to create a diversion.

Suddenly the woman starts shouting at the guards. Both turn toward her. Without hesitation, you draw your combat knife and do what you have to do. In just a few seconds, both guards are dead.

"They just took one of the other hostages up to be killed," cries the woman. "Hurry and you can catch them!"

To go after the hostage, turn to page **39.**

To remain here, turn to page **41.**

Snipers are trained to take out targets with one shot.

There's not much time. If you can kill one of the terrorists, you might create enough confusion to save the hostage. "Take the shot," you order.

The sound of the M24 sniper rifle echoes over the desert floor. One enemy jerks and falls. As you had hoped, the others seem to panic. Two of them hit the ground, covering their heads. Two more dash back toward the compound. You see one of them fall before you realize that Jones has fired another shot.

But your hopes are dashed when you notice the fifth terrorist has drawn a gun. Before Jones can fire a third shot, you see a flash from the end of the terrorist's pistol. The hostage slumps, dead.

"Hostage down!" you shout. "Move in!"

Your men move with amazing speed as they storm the compound. You don't have the element of surprise anymore. The terrorists know you're coming. You can't give them any extra time to organize.

Jones opens fire from behind, taking out both guards at the front gate. Next he manages to wound one of the enemy snipers on the roof. But the other slips inside to safety.

Jones' cover fire allows the rest of your team to approach safely. You smash through the gate and kick in the door of the compound.

The hallways are narrow and dark. Using only hand gestures, you order Martinez to take half the men down one hall. You lead the rest down the other. It doesn't take long to find the enemy. Suddenly you're in a heavy firefight. But your training, tactics, and weapons are superior. In just a few minutes, all of the terrorists are dead.

But so are Martinez and two of the hostages. Your medic tries desperately to save them, but there's nothing he can do. It was not a completely successful mission, but at least you managed to save three of the hostages. You will take the time to mourn the loss of your friend later. For now, you can only think about getting these people back to safety.

THE END

To follow another path, turn to page 11.
To read the conclusion, turn to page 101.

Storming the compound is your best option. "Move in," you command.

Your men don't hesitate. They trust you and follow your orders without question. You have to act quickly. The terrorists are focused on preparing the execution, which allows you to approach the compound unseen.

Half of the team opens fire on the guards at the front gate. You and the others climb over the chain-link fence that surrounds the compound.

As your boots hit the ground, you draw your M4A1 carbine rifle. A terrorist holds a pistol to the hostage's head. But before he can pull the trigger, you stop him with a single shot. You don't take the time to watch the man slump to the ground. You've already trained your rifle on another enemy.

Turn the page.

By this time your men have joined you. It's not much of a fight. The terrorists are confused and disorganized. The two at the gate are down, as well as the two on the roof. Within moments only your men and the terrified hostage remain outside. You rush to his side and untie him. His face is bloodied and bruised, but he's not seriously wounded.

The hostage tells you that at least five more terrorists are inside. The rest of the hostages are being held in a basement room.

You lead six of your men into the compound. Knowing that the hostages are downstairs, you go in firing. The terrorists inside never have a chance. As you clear the top floor, Martinez goes to the hostages downstairs. When the smoke clears, every terrorist is dead, and you haven't lost a single hostage. They're battered, bruised, and frightened, but they're OK.

As you call in a helicopter to evacuate your men and the hostages, Martinez pats you on the back. You're grateful that your mission was a success.

The Army green beret is a symbol of courage and dedication.

THE END

To follow another path, turn to page 11.
To read the conclusion, turn to page 101.

Green Berets are skilled in urban combat techniques.

There's no way you're setting down your weapon in a combat situation. You have only one choice. You have to take the shot.

Quickly you raise your Beretta M9 pistol and fire. The shot hits the enemy squarely between the eyes. He topples over, releasing the hostage, who rushes to your side.

"Where are the others?" you shout over the gunfire echoing through the halls.

The hostage is beaten and bruised. You can see he's terrified. But he's also strong. "Follow me," he says.

The man leads you down a flight of stairs. "There are two guards inside," he warns. "Probably one on each side of the door."

You nod and motion him to step back into the hall. Then you kick in the door. You step inside with your rifle and fire a shot at the startled terrorist sitting inside. Instantly you dive to the ground and roll, searching for the second guard. He's right where the hostage said he'd be. Before he can react, you fire a second shot. Just like that, both guards are dead.

Turn the page.

Three hostages remain inside. You untie them and make sure none are seriously injured. You grab your radio and tell Martinez that you've secured the hostages. "My men will clear out the upper level," you tell the frightened hostages. "We'll have you out of here in no time."

Within minutes, the sound of gunfire fades away. Your men have done their job. You've saved four of the five hostages. Many would consider that a success. But not you. Your job was to rescue all five, and you failed to do so. You promise yourself you'll do better next time.

THE END

To follow another path, turn to page 11.
To read the conclusion, turn to page 101.

You've probably already lost at least one hostage. You can't risk the life of another. You don't want to lay down your weapon. Instead you hold it out in front of your body, pointed away from the terrorist.

"Easy now," you say. "We can talk this out. Why don't you start by letting go of the hostage?"

Before you realize what has happened, you hear a shot. You feel the strength in your legs suddenly leave you. You slump to the ground, noticing a strange feeling in your abdomen. You clutch your stomach and look down. Your hands are covered in blood. The terrorist shot you!

Dimly, you're aware of the terrorist turning his gun toward the hostage. You're losing blood quickly. You have only a few moments to regret your decision. You should have known better. The man was cornered. He knew there was no escape.

Turn the page.

The battle is far from over, but your part in it is done. You can only hope the rest of your team and the hostages will make it out alive. You know that you won't.

THE END

To follow another path, turn to page 11.
To read the conclusion, turn to page 101.

You've saved four hostages, but your mission is to bring back all five. "What's your name?" you ask the hostage who helped you. She seems the least panicked of the bunch.

"Sarah," she answers.

"Sarah, take this." You hand her the pistol. "If any terrorists come down those stairs, you know what to do."

Sarah nods. Her hands are shaking, but she doesn't flinch at the thought of firing the weapon.

You detach your M4A1 carbine and charge up the stairs and down the hallway. You round a corner and spot two people in the distance. One is dragging the other through a door.

You sprint down the hallway and out the door. You're standing in a large garage. The hostage shouts as he sees you. Moments later, gunshots echo off the garage walls.

Turn the page.

Lucky for you, the terrorist is a bad shot. You drop to the ground and roll behind a workbench. You spot the terrorist ducking behind a jeep. The hostage is free, but that won't matter unless you kill or capture the enemy.

The terrorist fires again. You then hear a clicking sound. His ammo clip is empty! You're on your feet in a flash. Before the enemy can reload, you're on him. He reaches for a knife, but you don't give him the chance. You smash his face with the butt of your weapon. He falls to the floor.

You stand and wipe the sweat from your brow. You've managed to save all five hostages and take a prisoner in the process. Not a bad day's work for an elite U.S. Army Special Forces team.

THE END

To follow another path, turn to page 11.
To read the conclusion, turn to page 101.

You have four people here. You're not about to leave them undefended. You grab your radio and inform your men of the situation. A minute later you hear the sounds of gunfire from above. The compound then falls into an eerie silence.

Your radio squawks. Martinez gives you the report. The terrorist is dead, but he managed to kill the hostage first. The terrorist shot Hicks in the shoulder as well. Hicks should survive, but he won't be going out on missions anytime soon.

You've saved four of the hostages, but somehow the mission doesn't feel like a success.

THE END

To follow another path, turn to page 11.
To read the conclusion, turn to page 101.

Helicopters such as the MH-6 carry Rangers to mission sites.

CHAPTER 3

Rangers Lead the Way

The mission: Airborne assault

Objective: Seize control of an airstrip deep in enemy territory. Hold the airstrip until reinforcements arrive.

The enemy: At least 100 soldiers armed with heavy machine guns, rocket-propelled grenades, and anti-aircraft missiles.

Rules of engagement: Use deadly force as needed.

"Lieutenant, one minute until insertion," says the pilot of the UH-60 Black Hawk helicopter.

"Acknowledged," you reply.

Turn the page.

Rangers use fast ropes to descend from helicopters.

You're the leader of a platoon of Army Rangers with an important mission. The Army is planning an invasion. It needs to gain control of an enemy airstrip to transport troops and supplies. Your platoon's job is to seize the airstrip and stamp out any enemy resistance.

You and the 35 Rangers under your command are ready. As the four Black Hawks carrying your men hover over the insertion point, you drop fast ropes out the door. You and your team zip down the ropes to the ground.

Within minutes, your men are organized and ready to attack. The Black Hawks turn and zoom away.

People sometimes call the Rangers shock troops. Your motto is "Army Rangers lead the way." You're about to demonstrate why. Your mission is to hit the enemy hard, using surprise as your ally.

The airstrip is well defended. You'll need to take out the enemy's heavy weapons and capture or kill the enemy soldiers. Only then will it be safe for U.S. aircraft to use the airstrip.

Turn the page.

Your men move toward the target. You stay behind the cover of a long ridge running along the south end of the strip. Your first priority is to take out the enemy forces. Several enemy soldiers are patrolling the area around the airstrip. But most are grouped near a small hangar at one end of the strip.

To order snipers to take out the patrols, go to page **47**.

To order an assault on the hangar, turn to page **49**.

"We need to take out those patrols first," you tell the three squad leaders under your command. "Warrant Officer Chen, take your squad to the ridge and eliminate the targets."

You and the other two squads prepare for the attack. Within minutes Warrant Officer Brian Chen and his snipers are set. You watch through binoculars as Chen begins the attack. The sharp pops of M24 sniper rifles echo over the ridge. One by one, the enemy patrol soldiers fall. Chen's snipers don't miss a single shot.

Ranger teams wait for the precise moment to strike.

But the enemy has also heard the shots. "The main force is organizing," reports one of your Rangers. "They know we're coming."

You've lost the element of surprise, which means this mission just got a lot more dangerous. You could fire rocket-propelled grenades (RPGs) into the enemy forces. However, the RPGs could also damage the airstrip, which you can't let happen. The only other option is a dangerous assault on a prepared enemy.

"What are your orders, sir?" asks Warrant Officer Noah Hernandez.

To fire RPGs at the enemy, turn to page 51.

To launch an assault, turn to page 54.

"The patrols aren't a major concern," you say. "We need to hit the main force hard before they can organize and defend themselves. Warrant Officer Hernandez, any recommendations?"

Noah Hernandez is one of your squad leaders. He's an experienced Ranger who has seen his share of combat. You trust his instincts.

"The ridge will give us cover most of the way to the hangar," he says. "We follow it and keep the element of surprise. Leave a few men back to lay down cover fire as we move in hard. Don't give the enemy a chance to organize."

Warrant Officer Brian Chen steps up. "If we hit them with rocket-propelled grenades first, they'll be confused and disorganized. We could sweep in and clean them out before they even realize what hit them."

Turn the page.

Chen makes a good point. Firing RPGs first would almost certainly make the attack safer for you and your men. But using RPGs could put the mission in jeopardy. You can't afford to damage the airstrip. The U.S. military needs it in order to hold this territory.

Your men stand waiting. It's your choice.

To fire RPGs at the enemy, go to page **51**.

To storm the enemy forces, turn to page **56**.

It's risky, but the chance to cripple the enemy without losing a single man is too tempting to resist.

You lead two squads along the ridge, toward the airstrip. As soon as you're in position, Chen orders his men to fire.

You watch as several Rangers hoist the shoulder-mounted weapons, take aim, and fire. Trails of smoke follow the rockets as they scream toward their targets.

The first RPG slams into the hangar. The explosion takes out almost an entire wall. The enemy has no time to react. Within seconds a second blast erupts, and then a third. Black smoke rises from the hangar. You're sure that many of the enemy troops are already wounded or dead.

Turn the page.

The RPG-7 shoots grenades at targets up to 1,600 feet away.

You prepare to order your troops in. But before you can, one last RPG speeds toward the hangar. It sails high and smashes directly into the paved airstrip, leaving a huge crater. You groan—your commanding officers are not going to like that.

There's no time to worry about that now, though. You order your men to charge. The enemy is wounded and confused. You notice a group of about six enemy soldiers trying to organize a resistance. They're swinging a heavy machine gun in your direction. You can't allow them to open fire on your men.

*To charge the heavy machine gun yourself, turn to page **62**.*

*To order your men to secure the weapon, turn to page **64**.*

"Move in," you order. The enemy knows you're here now. Any further delay could prove deadly.

Your men are ready. As you and your two squads charge forward, Chen's squad continues to fire. The snipers give you some protection, but the enemy has had time to organize.

You're under heavy fire as you approach the hangar. You spot several enemy troop carriers parked about 100 feet from the hangar. It's the only cover you have, so you lead your men behind the armored vehicles.

The firefight is intense. You watch as half a dozen enemy soldiers go down. But your men are suffering as well. Three have been wounded. At least one is dead. Suddenly an explosion shakes the ground. An enemy grenade has exploded near your position. You see at least five more wounded Rangers. The enemy is moving toward you.

Rangers train with smoke canisters to prepare for battle situations.

Your remaining men look to you. You can't hesitate. You open your mouth and shout:

"Retreat! Fall back!", turn to page **66**.

"Advance! Full attack!", turn to page **68**.

Hernandez has the right idea. Your men are the best-trained combat soldiers in the world. Combine that with the element of surprise, and you feel sure of victory. There's no good reason to risk damaging the valuable airstrip with heavy RPG fire.

You lead all three squads along the ridge, out of sight of the enemy soldiers. Finally it's time to charge. You send Chen and a few of his squad members to the top of the ridge. Then you give the rest of the Rangers the order to attack. The moment the enemy spots you, Chen and his men will lay down cover fire.

As you charge, you notice two main targets. They are the enemy's command center and a group of heavy weapons, including machine guns and artillery. If you can take out the enemy's command center, the remaining soldiers will be disorganized and likely to surrender.

But on the other hand, the heavy weapons seem like a much bigger immediate threat. You would hate to see those guns turned against your men. Even an elite Army Ranger is no match for a heavy machine gun.

Ranger Special Operations Vehicles (RSOVs) can carry machine guns.

To focus your efforts on the command center, turn to page **58.**

To order your men to take out the weapons, turn to page **60.**

"Take out the command center," you order.

Your men respond immediately, focusing their fire. You see at least two enemy officers go down.

The enemy soldiers seem to sense how desperate the situation is. They push back hard. A grenade explodes only 20 feet from your position. Several of your men are wounded.

You realize that without cover, your men are too exposed. The only cover you can see is a group of enemy troop carriers parked to one side of the hangar.

"Get to the troop carriers!" you shout.

Several more Rangers fall. By now both sides have suffered heavy losses. The firefight rages on.

You hear the roar of a heavy machine gun. It sprays your position with a swarm of large-caliber rounds. You don't have any defense against such heavy weaponry. You've already lost the battle. The only question that remains is what you should do.

To order a retreat, turn to page 66.

To order a full attack, turn to page 68.

Taking out the command center is important, but disarming the enemy has to be your first priority. You shout over the rattle of gunfire, pointing toward the heavy machine guns.

Your men understand and react immediately. Enemy soldiers are frantically trying to swing the weapons in your direction, but your Rangers don't give them time.

The sound of your M249 Squad Automatic Weapons (SAWs) fills the air as you advance on the enemy force. Your men are all expert marksmen. The enemy soldiers fall before they can return fire. A Ranger tosses a grenade toward the guns, disabling them. Problem solved!

With the heavy weapons destroyed, you turn your attention to the command center. The enemy is confused and panicked. Your men advance on the center. Most of the remaining enemy soldiers lay down their weapons. They know they've lost.

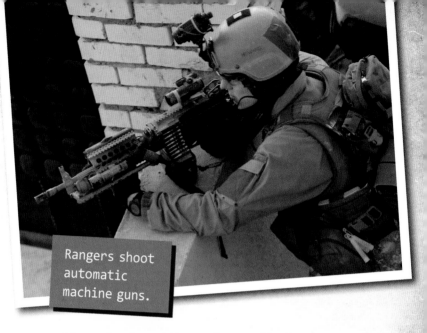

Rangers shoot automatic machine guns.

You take the soldiers prisoner. You're sure your commanding officers will want to question them.

The airstrip is secure. One of your Rangers took a bullet in the leg, but he'll be fine. The rest of your men have come through without a scratch. It was close to a perfect mission. You couldn't be more proud to be a member of the Army Rangers.

THE END

To follow another path, turn to page 11.
To read the conclusion, turn to page 101.

You raise your M249 Squad Automatic Weapon (SAW) and charge at the machine gun. As you squeeze the trigger, one of the enemies falls. The others turn to you, raising their weapons.

You hit the dirt and roll away from the fire. Once again, you raise your SAW and take a shot. Another enemy down. But now you're in trouble. There's no cover out here, and at least four enemy weapons are focused on you.

There's nowhere to retreat, so you charge instead. Your bold move catches the enemy soldiers off guard. You manage to wound another, but suddenly your right leg gives out from under you. You've been shot! You fall hard to the ground as your SAW slips from your hands.

Two remaining enemies are moving toward you, guns pointed. You know they'll kill you. But you have one last surprise. You grab your Beretta M9 pistol, raise it, and squeeze off a single shot.

It's the last shot you'll ever fire. But before a bullet ends your life, you have the satisfaction of knowing that your final shot hit home. That's one less enemy the rest of your Rangers will have to worry about.

THE END

To follow another path, turn to page 11.
To read the conclusion, turn to page 101.

You have to act quickly. "Hernandez!" you shout over the sound of gunfire, pointing toward the heavy machine gun.

Hernandez understands. He alerts three of his squad members. The five of you open fire on the enemy soldiers. They're down before they even realize what hit them.

"Disable that weapon," you order. You don't stick around to see it happen. Hernandez and his men are Army Rangers. They'll get the job done.

The enemy resistance is dying out. About half the enemy soldiers have laid down their weapons. Many others are dead. Smoke rises over the battle site. The sounds of gunfire are replaced by the moaning of the wounded men.

You order your men to begin taking prisoners. Your commanding officers will be eager to question them about the enemy's defenses.

There's still plenty of work to do. But the hard part is over. You've secured the airstrip, but it's damaged. You can only hope that your reinforcements will still be able to use it.

Rangers work together to open fire on an enemy target.

THE END

To follow another path, turn to page 11.
To read the conclusion, turn to page 101.

You're beaten. The enemy has every advantage. Your only hope is to fall back behind the safety of the ridge and regroup.

Hernandez and three of the other wounded men can't walk. You won't be able to carry them out. "Lieutenant," Hernandez gasps, "get out of here. We've got you covered."

You start to argue with him, but realize he's right. These men can open fire on the enemy as you retreat. It might be enough to get you back to safety.

There's no time to waste. As Hernandez and his men lay down cover fire, the rest of you rush back to the safety of the ridge. Two men fall during the retreat, but a dozen survive. You know that without the sacrifice of Hernandez and his men, no one would have made it out alive. You promise yourself that you'll never forget what they did for you.

The battle is lost. All you can do now is call in a helicopter to get your men back to safety. You have failed, and your orders have left many brave Rangers dead. You'll have to live with that for the rest of your life.

THE END

To follow another path, turn to page 11.
To read the conclusion, turn to page 101.

You're doomed if you stay here. The enemy
is growing bolder by the moment. As you shout
out the attack order, your men spring into action.
You rush around both sides of the troop carriers,
weapons raised. You charge at the hangar.

For a moment the maneuver seems to catch
the enemy off guard. Several enemy soldiers fall
back in panic. But most of them hold their ground.
You gambled that the enemy would be too afraid
to stand against a Ranger assault. You've lost
that gamble.

The space between the troop carriers and the
hangar is a war zone. Guns fire, men fall and die,
and explosions rock the ground. You're less than 50
yards from the hangar when an enemy bullet tears
into your shoulder. The impact spins you around.

You crash to the ground, but you never let go of your M249 Squad Automatic Weapon (SAW). You keep firing shots at the enemy until the last moment. But the outcome of this battle has long since been decided. You have lost, and now you're bleeding to death. You only hope that some of your men have better luck than you.

THE END

To follow another path, turn to page 11.
To read the conclusion, turn to page 101.

SEALs perform missions
in the sea, in the air,
and on land.

CHAPTER 4

Sea, Land, and Air

The mission: Counterterrorism

Objective: Capture the terrorist leader whose code name is the Viper.

The enemy: Little is known of the Viper or the forces that surround him except that they want to destroy the United States.

Rules of engagement: Use deadly force as needed to capture the Viper.

Aboard a U.S. Navy aircraft carrier, you study the maps spread out before you. You're the leader of a small, elite Navy SEAL squad. You've been called to perform a dangerous and top-secret mission.

Turn the page.

Agent Carla Stevens of the Central Intelligence Agency (CIA) briefs you on the situation.

"We have reliable intelligence that a massive terrorist attack on the United States is going to happen," she says. "But we don't know just how or where. We do know that the terrorist known as the Viper is behind the plot."

Stevens hands you a photo. The Viper is about 30 years old and has a large brown mole on his left cheek.

Stevens gives you another photo. "This is a satellite image of his location." It shows a mansion located on a remote coast. The shoreline is littered with jagged rocks. A tall fence surrounds the other three sides of the large house. Only a single dirt road leads to the house's front gate.

"The Viper is in this building," she says. "You and your team must get inside and capture him. Questioning him is our only chance to prevent this attack. Good luck, Lieutenant."

Reaching the target will be difficult. You could have a Chinook helicopter drop you nearby and approach by land, or you could approach by sea.

To approach by land, turn to page **74**.

To approach by sea, turn to page **76**.

SEALs dangle from fast ropes that are as long as 90 feet.

That night you and the seven SEALs in your squad climb aboard a Chinook helicopter. The chopper flies low to avoid being seen. A few miles from the target site, it hovers just above the rugged shoreline. You and your men throw down fast ropes and slide down to the ground. The Chinook lifts, turns, and disappears into the night sky.

You move on foot toward the target area. Within an hour, it's in sight. You use night-vision goggles to view the darkened mansion. You spot one guard at the gate and a second on the roof. You also see movement inside the house.

"There's only one man watching the fence," says Warrant Officer Ben Thompson, your second-in-command. "If we move fast and quiet, we should be able to climb the fence undetected."

"If only one man guards the gate, we could go in the front," says Petty Officer Greg Yates. "It would be easier."

He's right. But you'd also be risking letting the enemy know you're here. The men are looking at you, waiting for your order.

To crash the gate, turn to page **78**.

To sneak over the fence, turn to page **80**.

SEALs are expert swimmers, even when loaded with weapons and gear.

You feel the chop of the waves as you and your men cruise toward your target in a Rigid Inflatable Boat (RIB). It's midnight and the ocean is dark. The low hum of the boat's engine is muffled by the sound of the crashing waves.

The boat's pilot pulls up several hundred feet short of the rocky coast. You can see the lights of the mansion in the distance. Your RIB blends into the darkness. Nobody will know you're here.

"This is it," says the boat's pilot. It's as far as the RIB will take you.

"Let's go," you tell your men. The eight of you slip quietly into the water. The sea is rough, but you're all expert swimmers. That's part of being a SEAL. You reach the rocky coast and climb your way up. You gather behind a large boulder to brief the men.

"One man on the roof," you say.

Warrant Officer Ben Thompson, your second-in-command, puts a hand on your arm. "Lieutenant," he whispers, pointing. Someone is headed in your direction! You peer around the boulder. The person appears to be a guard. He is carrying an automatic rifle but doesn't seem to realize you're here. This is probably a routine patrol.

To attack the man, turn to page **81**.

To remain hidden, turn to page **82**.

SEALs can quickly move from water to land missions.

"We'll crash the gate," you order. It's just one guard, and you'll catch him by surprise.

You move along the fence as you approach the gate, sticking to the shadows. The guard sits in a small shack outside the iron gate. He appears to be reading, rather than watching the gate. You could just shoot him, but it would be better to take him out silently. You might even be able to get him to tell you where the Viper is.

You motion for your men to hang back as you approach. You have your combat knife in hand. But as you close the last few feet to the shack, the guard looks up. You can see he's frozen with fear. You sprint forward, ready to grab him. But the man recovers from his shock and raises his rifle.

You're too quick for him. You grab his arm before he can point his weapon at you. But he manages to squeeze the trigger. The noise of the shot rings through the air.

With one swift movement, you twist the man around and kill him. But it's too late. The enemy now knows you're here. Your job just became much harder.

Turn to page 83.

Thompson points to a dark area where you can move over the fence unnoticed. He tosses a rope over the fence. One by one you climb over the fence. You're the last one to clear it. When your boots hit the ground, you know you still have the element of surprise.

It's time to go inside. The longer you wait out here, the greater the chance you'll be spotted.

"Remember, we need the Viper alive," you remind your men. "Shoot to kill for the others, but take no risks with him. Let's do this."

Turn to page 85.

You point at Thompson and then at the approaching guard. Then you put your finger to your lips. You don't need to speak—he knows exactly what you're ordering him to do.

As the guard passes your position, Thompson draws his combat knife and sneaks out from behind the boulder. He grabs the man from behind. He then slips his hand over the guard's mouth to prevent him from shouting. Thompson tries to disable the man, but the guard manages to squirm free. He spins and raises his automatic rifle.

You don't let him get the shot. In a heartbeat, you've raised your own M4A1 assault rifle and squeezed the trigger. The guard slumps to the ground. Thompson is fine, but the sound of gunfire has surely alerted the enemy that you're here. You've lost the element of surprise. That's not good news.

Turn to page 83.

Without a word, you signal your men to stay down. You can't afford to be spotted yet. The guard is walking slowly, not seeming very alert. That confirms your idea that this is just a routine patrol. If you can stay unseen, you stand a much better chance of success.

The guard walks by. He passes within a few yards of your position, but he doesn't see you. Chief Petty Officer Ted Gordon, the senior enlisted man on the team, whispers, "We could take him out right here. One less terrorist to fight later."

It's true. The fewer terrorists, the easier your mission would be. But is it worth the risk of raising an alarm?

To wait for the guard to clear out and continue on to the mansion, turn to page 85.

To try to take out the guard, turn to page 97.

The M4A1 rifle can shoot up to 950 rounds of ammunition per minute.

The enemy's alarm has gone up. Now you have to act quickly. "Let's go!" you shout. You and your men rush toward the mansion. You kick in the door and sweep inside, your M4A1 rifles raised.

The enemy fires on you as soon as you enter the building. But they're still disorganized, and you have better weapons. With just a few shots, your men take out the shooters. You press forward until you come to a staircase.

Turn the page.

"Thompson, Yates, Gordon, Peters—upstairs," you order. The four SEALs charge up the stairs. You, Anderson, Scott, and Abdullah sweep the lower level. You'll search every corner of this mansion until you find the Viper.

You move up and down empty hallways. You hear gunfire from upstairs, but it lasts only a moment. The house suddenly seems very quiet. You search the rooms one by one, finding nothing. Anderson then kicks in a door that leads to a garage. As he does, you hear the roar of a truck engine come to life.

Two men sit in the truck's cab. You instantly recognize one of the men. It's the Viper—he's trying to escape! The truck's tires squeal as it heads out the garage door.

To try to stop the truck by firing at its tires, turn to page 87.

To throw yourself in front of the truck to block its path, turn to page 90.

Keeping the element of surprise is the best option. The eight of you move silently along one side of the mansion. You're in luck when you spot an open window on the ground floor. The room inside is dark and empty. It's a perfect entry point.

"Thompson, Yates, Gordon, Peters, stay outside and cover the exits," you order. "Anderson, Scott, and Abdullah, you're with me."

You slip inside through the window and then move into a well-lit hallway. Voices are coming from one of the rooms. You silently move outside the door and use a small mirror to peer inside.

Three men are seated inside the room. You instantly recognize one of them as the Viper. An open door stands at the far end of the room. It appears to lead into a garage. You motion to your men. You and Scott will go in together. Anderson and Abdullah will guard the doorway behind you.

Turn the page.

Your attack is so sudden that the terrorists barely have time to respond. You and Petty Officer Evan Scott storm into the room. Scott raises his M4A1 rifle and immediately shoots one of the men in the chest. The other reaches for a weapon as the Viper stands and bolts for the far door.

To shoot the Viper in the leg, turn to page **92.**

To turn and fire on the armed man, turn to page **95.**

SEALs are trained to use deadly force when necessary.

"Stop that truck!" you order. You raise your rifle and fire at one of the front tires. Your men take out two of the other tires. Within moments the truck comes to a stop.

That's when you hear two gunshots. You're about to take cover when you realize that the enemy hasn't shot at you. The garage grows terribly silent as you realize what has happened.

Turn the page.

You rush to the truck and throw open the passenger side door. The Viper is slumped forward in the front seat. A bullet hole is in his forehead. The driver is dead as well. Both men knew you wanted to capture the Viper alive. They were willing to do anything to make sure you didn't succeed.

You still hope to recover important information from the mansion. Just then a massive explosion rocks the building behind you. You and your men hit the ground as shrapnel flies through the air.

You hear more explosions. The terrorists had rigged the house to explode to prevent you from collecting evidence!

You and your men gather outside. Several have been hit by shrapnel, but no one is seriously wounded. The house is engulfed in flames.

You and your men have survived, and a dangerous terrorist leader is dead. But otherwise the mission has been a terrible failure. You can only hope that the CIA finds another way to stop the upcoming terrorist attack.

THE END

To follow another path, turn to page 11.
To read the conclusion, turn to page 101.

You throw yourself in front of the truck, pointing your rifle at the cab. But the driver doesn't slow down. He's called your bluff—you can't fire, or you'll risk killing the Viper. You dive from the truck's path at the last moment.

The truck squeals out of the garage. You and your men chase after it. But before you get outside, a huge explosion rocks the mansion. The terrorists must have set off a bomb rigged up inside the house! Bits of sharp metal shrapnel fly through the air. They hit your face, abdomen, and legs. You collapse to the ground.

The garage is filled with thick black smoke. Somewhere you hear one of your men moaning. You try to stand but realize that you can't feel your legs. You're becoming lightheaded. You look down at your shaking hand and see it covered in blood.

You're hurt badly. Your squad mates are wounded or dead. And there's no help on the way. As the Viper is making his escape, you're taking your last breath. The mission has failed. That failure has cost you your life.

THE END

To follow another path, turn to page 11.
To read the conclusion, turn to page 101.

You raise your weapon and fire at the Viper. You're careful with your aim—you can't risk hitting a vital organ. Instead you hit him in the lower leg. The Viper screams as he falls to the floor. A pistol falls out of his reach.

The other man fires a shot, but in his hurry, his aim is bad. The bullet grazes your left arm. That will hurt later, but right now you don't even feel the pain. You turn to return fire, but Scott is one step ahead of you. He puts a bullet in the man's chest. The man collapses to the floor, dead.

At that moment, you hear gunfire from outside the mansion. Your men are taking out other terrorists as they flee the building. You trust them to do their job as you rush to the Viper. His leg is bleeding, but it's not a life-threatening wound. You tear a strip of fabric from his shirt and tightly wrap it above the wound.

Search-and-rescue missions are part of SEAL training.

You and your men carry the Viper outside. The
mansion has been secured. Six terrorists are dead.
Two others have been taken prisoner. You grab your
radio and call for a helicopter pickup. The CIA
will comb the house for evidence, but you have the
biggest prize already. The Viper is in custody. You
know the CIA will do whatever it takes to get the
information they need from the man.

"Nice work, Lieutenant," says Thompson as you watch the Chinook helicopter touch down. You give him a quick smile. Your team performed the mission flawlessly. The United States is safer for the work you've done here tonight.

THE END

To follow another path, turn to page 11.
To read the conclusion, turn to page 101.

You whirl and fire at the armed man. Your shot catches him in the shoulder but doesn't take him down. He fires, and you hear Scott groan. The bullet has caught him in the abdomen.

You slam the butt of your rifle into the terrorist's face. He falls to the floor, unconscious.

The Viper has used those precious seconds to flee into the garage. You hear a truck's engine fire up and the squeal of tires on the pavement. You grab your radio and tell your men outside to stop the truck.

Seconds later you hear the sounds of gunfire. You race outside, leaving Abdullah with Scott to help him tend to his wound. Your men are firing on the truck as it crashes through the gate. But while their shots hit the truck, they don't stop it. It speeds away on the narrow dirt road that leads away from the mansion. The Viper is escaping!

Turn the page.

You quickly grab your radio and report the situation. The Navy will be able to scramble helicopters to try to chase down the target. But there are no guarantees. Your mission was to capture the Viper, and you've failed to do that. All you can do is hope someone else succeeds where you have failed.

THE END

To follow another path, turn to page 11.
To read the conclusion, turn to page 101.

You don't like the idea of killing a man this way, but this is war. The safety of your nation depends on your success. You'll stop at nothing to defend it.

"Gordon's right," you whisper. "One less terrorist to get in our way later. Gordon, you're with me. Everyone else, move on my order."

Silently you and Gordon move out from behind the boulder. You don't want to shoot the man, since gunfire would raise an alarm. You draw your combat knife instead.

"Cover me," you say to Gordon.

He raises his rifle and takes a shooting position. You know he won't fire unless it's absolutely necessary. But with what you have planned, that shouldn't be a problem.

Turn the page.

SEALs follow a code of never leaving another SEAL behind.

As quietly as you can, you close the distance behind the guard. He's not paying much attention and never sees you coming. You grab him and give him a fatal wound. But he manages to fire his weapon before he dies. Within seconds, a floodlight comes on, lighting up the entire area. You hear shouting. Before you can take cover, you hear a shot. You gasp for breath as you fall to the ground. A guard on the roof has shot you in the gut. Blood oozes from your wound.

In the distance, you hear more gunfire and shouting. As you lie there dying, you realize that your men have been spotted. You can only hope their SEAL training allows them to make it out alive. You know the mission is a failure. You have paid for that failure with your life.

THE END

To follow another path, turn to page 11.
To read the conclusion, turn to page 101.

Navy SEALs and other Special Ops soldiers are among the best in the world.

CHAPTER 5

Elite Warriors

The Special Forces are the elite warriors of the U.S. military. There's little they can't do. Whether it's gathering secret intelligence on an enemy, rescuing hostages, attacking enemy strongholds, or defeating terrorist plots, the Special Forces have done it.

They're an important part of any combat situation and especially key in the war on terror. They help make the U.S. military the most powerful in the world. They represent the best of the U.S. armed forces with their dedication, fearlessness, and intelligence.

Soldiers hone their skills in events such as the Best Ranger Competition.

Do you have what it takes to be an elite Special Forces warrior? It's no easy task. To make it, you have to be tough, both mentally and physically. You'll have to work hard and endure intense years of specialized training. That takes a level of dedication that few people have.

You'll have to be prepared to push your mind and body beyond their natural limits. And of course, you will need to be prepared to lay your life on the line to defend your country. Does any of that sound easy? Of course not. They don't call them the ordinary forces. They're called special for a reason.

The job of a Special Forces member is unlike any other in the world. Any choice you make means the difference between success and failure, between life and death—your own, that of your fellow troops, or of innocent civilians.

So what do you think? Do you thrive under pressure? Are you willing to do whatever it takes to protect the United States and its allies? If so, you just might have what it takes to be a member of the U.S. Special Forces.

Timeline

1756–American Major Robert Rogers organizes the first group of Army Rangers to fight for the British in the French and Indian War; soldiers known as Rangers also fight in the Revolutionary War, the War of 1812, and the Civil War.

1941–1945–The World War II Office of Strategic Services sends highly trained troops behind enemy lines to help resistance movements against the enemy; these types of soldiers later become known as Green Berets.

1950–The Army establishes a Ranger training school at Fort Benning, Georgia; successful graduates of the school fight in the Korean War.

1961–President John F. Kennedy authorizes the formation of Special Forces teams in all military branches.

1977–Army Colonel Charlie Beckwith forms Delta Force, a secret unit of Special Forces soldiers.

1980–Delta Force takes part in its first mission, Operation Eagle Claw, a failed attempt to rescue American hostages held at the U.S. Embassy in Tehran, Iran; the 160th Special Operations Aviation Regiment (Airborne) is formed; the group is better known as the Night Stalkers.

1983–Various Special Forces groups work together to capture the small Caribbean island nation of Grenada after its military overthrows its government.

1987–The U.S. Special Operations Command forms to oversee all of the U.S. military's special forces.

1989–Army Rangers lead the charge in Operation Just Cause, an invasion in Panama to remove dictator Manuel Noriega from office.

2002–Special Forces soldiers help carry out Operation Anaconda and take out a terrorist stronghold in Afghanistan.

2011–A SEAL team locates and kills terrorist leader Osama bin Laden in Pakistan.

2012–A SEAL team rescues two hostages in Somalia.

REAL MISSIONS

2012, Somalia

Navy SEALS parachuted into an area near the town of
Adado. The SEALs walked two miles to a compound
where two aid workers, one of them American, were
being held hostage. The SEALs killed at least eight of the
kidnappers and rescued the two hostages unharmed.

2011, Pakistan

Chinook helicopters carried a team of Navy SEALs to a
house in Pakistan. Intelligence had revealed that terrorist
leader Osama bin Laden was living inside the house. The
SEALs stormed the complex. They killed bin Laden and
other terrorists in the building and recovered valuable
intelligence on bin Laden's terrorist group, al-Qaeda.

2009, Somalia

Somali pirates captured cargo ship Captain Richard Phillips in the Indian Ocean off the coast of Somalia. The pirates threatened to kill Phillips, so the Navy sent SEALs to rescue him. The SEALs first tried to negotiate with the pirates. But they soon realized that Phillips was in great danger from the three pirates holding him. Three SEAL snipers took aim on a choppy sea and killed the pirates. Phillips was rescued.

2001, Afghanistan

Green Berets began training troops in Afghanistan's Northern Alliance. The Alliance troops opposed the Taliban government, an enemy of the United States. The Green Berets taught Alliance fighters new ways to resist the Taliban. By training the Alliance troops, the Green Berets gave the U.S. military a more powerful ally in the war to bring down the Taliban government.

REAL MISSIONS

1994, Panama

Members of Delta Force and the U.S. Army Night
Stalkers carried out Operation Acid Gambit. The Night
Stalkers landed helicopters on the roof of a prison in
Panama. The Deltas stormed the prison, shot a guard, and
rescued American Kurt Muse, a CIA operative being held
there. As the soldiers and Muse escaped, their helicopter
crashed. The Deltas rushed everyone into a nearby
building and held it until a troop carrier arrived to take
them to safety.

1983, Grenada

Two Army Ranger battalions led Operation Urgent
Fury, the U.S. invasion of Grenada. The military of the
small island nation near Venezuela had overthrown its
government. The Rangers used parachutes to land on the
southern half of the island. Despite heavy resistance, the
Rangers rescued American medical school students and
secured several important locations, including the Point
Salines Airfield.

READ MORE

Hunter, Nick. *Military Survival.* Chicago: Raintree, 2011.

Montana, Jack. *Navy SEALs.* Broomall, Pa.: Mason Crest Publishers, 2011.

Nelson, Drew. *Green Berets.* New York: Gareth Stevens Pub., 2012.

Vanderhoof, Gabrielle, and C. F. Earl. *Army Rangers.* Broomall, Pa.: Mason Crest Publishers, 2011.

INTERNET SITES

Use FactHound to find Internet sites related to this book. All of the sites on FactHound have been researched by our staff.

Here's all you do:
Visit *www.facthound.com*
Type in this code: 9781429685825

GLOSSARY

covert (koh-VURT)—secret

elite (i-LEET)—having special advantages or talents

grenade (gruh-NAYD)—a small explosive device that is often thrown at enemy targets

hangar (HANG-ur)—a large building where airplanes are parked

hostage (HOSS-tij)—a person taken by force and held, often as a way to obtain something

informant (in-FOR-muhnt)—a person who gives information about another person or group

intelligence (in-TEL-uh-jenss)—secret information about an enemy's plans or actions

platoon (pluh-TOON)—a group of soldiers made up of two or more squads

shrapnel (SHRAP-nuhl)—pieces that have broken off from an explosive shell

sniper (SNY-pur)—a soldier trained to shoot at long-distance targets from a hidden place

terrorist (TER-ur-ist)—a person who uses violence and threats to achieve a political goal

BIBLIOGRAPHY

ArmyRanger.com. 28 March 2012.
www.armyranger.com

Bahmanyar, Mir. *Shadow Warriors: A History of the U.S. Army Rangers.* Oxford: Osprey, 2006.

GoArmy—Special Forces. 28 March 2012.
www.goarmy.com/special-forces.html

Landau, Alan M., et al. *U.S. Special Forces: Airborne Rangers, Delta Force, and U.S. Navy Seals.* Osceola, Wis.: MBI, 1999.

Moore, Robin. *The Green Berets: The Amazing Story of the U.S. Army's Elite Special Forces Unit.* New York: Skyhorse Pub., 2007.

United States Navy SWCC. 28 March 2012.
www.sealswcc.com

United States Special Operations Command.
28 March 2012. www.socom.mil/default.aspx

INDEX